After - <u>AMERICA 2000: Foundations For Generations</u>!

Comes Now

THE BALL DOCTRINE!

- Creating Peace and Prosperity In Every Nation -

by

Dennis Andrew Ball

2024 American Party Presidential Candidate

THIS BOOK IS DEDICATED TO THE

LIFE & LEGACY OF OUR 35TH

PRESIDENT OF THE UNITED STATES,

<u>JOHN FITZGERALD KENNEDY</u>

WHO'S LIFE WAS TRAGICALLY

TAKEN ONE FATAL AUTUMN DAY IN

DALLAS, TEXAS – NOVEMBER 22, 1963

OF THIS - THE 50TH ANNIVERSARY

THE BALL DOCTRINE

ISBN 13: 978-0615836447
ISBN 10: 0615836445

THE BALL DOCTRINE

"And So My Fellow Americans,

Ask Not What Your Country Can

Do For You - Ask What You Can

Do For Your Country"

President John Fitzgerald Kennedy

-Inaugural Quote-
January 20, 1961

THE BALL DOCTRINE

TABLE OF CONTENTS

THE BALL DOCTRINE

ACKNOWLEDGMENTS

To the Individuals who gave their
time that this title could be timely produced and
marketed for the benefit of all mankind -

Dennis Andrew Ball

PROLOGUE

"AND SO MY FELLOW AMERICANS,

THINK 1ST WHAT OUR COUNTRY HAS

BECOME; ACT & DO WHAT MUST BE

DONE!"

DENNIS ANDREW BALL - AOA NOMINATION

QUOTE FROM ACCEPTANCE SPEECH FOR

PRESIDENT OF THE UNITED STATES

SEPTEMBER 16, 2012

THE BALL DOCTRINE

1. <u>THE GLOBAL ECONOMIC CRISIS!</u>

And so it is and has become the reality of our World Economies that our World has engulfed itself in a Global Economic Crisis created by those most entrusted within business, labor and government to protect the earth's populations from a cataclysmic meltdown of enormous proportions!

Instincts tell us that our problems are not with the past but with the current and future populations for they hold the keys to correcting our mistakes by learning from those who sacrificed and struggled to make this nation a more perfect place by which to raise their families and live their lives.

Do we dare do any less by those who lived and died so that you and I could be free to enjoy their sacrifice for Freedom and the Union? It is within this context that the premise of The Ball Doctrine is born to show the Nation and the World the path to Global Prosperity and to every country the path to enduring peace amongst nations. That is the leadership role of the United States Of America and of which President Kennedy said "I do not shrink from this responsibility- I welcome it!"[1]

In the long history of the United States , Crisis has always seemed to define our national destiny as we as a people many times have been forced to confront our personal lives with the same vigor that challenged us to perform sacrificially for our children and our families.

Now, like then, America's people are again called upon to correct the problems of their generation to insure that both the current and future generations have a fighting chance not only to survive but succeed in the tasks of life to insure domestic tranquility for the common defense of the electorate

[1]*President John Fitzgerald Kennedy's Inaugural Address, January 20, 1961*

and for the well being of current generations by that which Americans have enjoyed.

It is in this tradition, The Ball Doctrine came forth to confront and interrupt the negative flow of domestic and international events forcing a positive change within the context of nations and human events for ourselves and our children.

From those brave patriots in the Winter of 1777 marshaled at Valley Forge, Pennsylvania by their sure will to live and the creation of over 2,000 huts to house and shelter a rag-tag militia into a Continental Army ready to do battle against the world's most formidable fighting force, The British Army.

It can be said, that the Commander-In-Chief, General George Washington and his staff created in a few short months the means to answer the ends of war by which the World has profited mightily by a City On A Hill, a new Jerusalem; a birth of freedom and liberty unmatched in all of World History. I ask, do we not owe a great allegiance to those throughout our history who have given their lives for the cause of Freedom?

As it was then, so it is today, America is again faced by Citizens' priorities of being Subjects of the State or Individuals governed by Constitutional mandate. The choice is ours to make for our current generation and those to come.

In Europe, the governments are afraid of its citizens but in America, it's citizens' are afraid of their government. This must change. America was not intended to be a debtor nation nor create an Imperial State of Indentured Servant hood upon America's middle class but that is what is occurring within a corporate global culture emanating from the United States of America. How long can this go on? The people demand answers for they had nothing to do with Social Elitism opposed to strong family values from which the founders were committed to seeing the nation preserved and protected.

Can we do any less to preserve and protect that which they fought and died for this country, America to preserve, protect and defend against all threats, both foreign and domestic?

I tell all of you, know that our future is in all of our hands. Europe is a ticking time bomb. Their Union of European nations is fragile at best and can be swept under by the slightest variance in economic factors that will impact the American economy. A global market supported by the United States dollar as the reserve currency of choice is in jeopardy because of the debt burden accumulated by the United States over the past 50 years. This will continue to be a problem for the Federal Reserve System until the means of production are created in order to satisfy the ends. 'Made in America' must once again become the main stay for American life for its Citizens and families. To do otherwise will place America as a debtor nation, something the founders warned against as if an invading army had succeeded without firing a shot!

Democracy is hard work and governing a nation equally as challenging.

The global economic crisis was created during the Clinton Administration and accelerated after 9/11.

THE BALL DOCTRINE

Factors that weighed into the collapse began on Wall Street with Investment Bankers courting Congress to support legislation making it possible for them to make real estate loans on derivative speculation and poor processing.

Included in this scenario came Fannie Mae and Freddie Mac, two quasi-government agencies similar to that of the role played by the Federal Reserve System to that of banking.

These two agencies became a back stop for bad loans Wall Street Bankers plotted to use and became accustom to using to back up the loans if they should fail. Some have called it Predatory Lending knowing that a high percentage of these loans would fail especially those that were structured on interest only payments to the lender.

THE BALL DOCTRINE

Contributing greatly to it was the fact that while a correction was needed, the financial system was experiencing a cataclysmic event that required the Federal Reserve to Bail Out the banks to avert a total economic meltdown of the American economy repeating the years of the Great Depression caused by greed and over indulgence by a Corporate Elite.

There is much blame to be shared by those in business, labor and government. This is also true in Europe who used the American model of derivative banking as their own to make home loans to their nation's citizens and people funded much by Wall Street bankers funded by the Federal Reserve System.

Much has been said to create "Bad Banks" to funnel bad real estate loans from the ones that were good. Then sell those assets at auction prices to spur

the correction at the same time reforming the system.
Because derivative banking was popular as a financial
instrument amongst financial institutions and markets,
it proved that abusive banking practices at the
expense of borrowers and taxpayers can and will
bring the world's economies to the brink of economic
disaster and collapse.

Since the end of the Clinton Administration,
repeal of the Glass-Steagall Act[2] by then President,
Bill Clinton proved to be a disaster in the hands of
Wall Street Bankers. This collapse made its way to
the highest offices of the land threatening America's
Credit Rating and the jobs stability vitally necessary
to support America's children and families. What had
protected Americans for 70 years against speculative
banking was gone by a pen stroke from Bill Clinton,

[2]Glass-Steagall Banking Act 1933-The Hoover Great Depression

THE BALL DOCTRINE

President of the United States.

What's even worse, since then the past and present administrations have failed to restore the Glass-Steagall Act to once again protect Americans and tax payers from their abusive behavior of derivative speculative banking as if the nation is ready to set itself up once again for an even greater collapse of the economic and global financial system! How long can this abuse go on? There must be Rules and they must be followed! "To Big To Jail" must be cut down to size. Accountability and transparency must once again become the norm; not the exception.

There are laws on the books waiting to be enforced by the Justice Department without the political will to enforce or do something about it. Crimes are committed without fear of accountability! Where are the Anti-trust; Anti-monopoly Trustees?

THE BALL DOCTRINE

2.   THE MORAL CRISIS!

And so it continues to manifest and seems to
mask itself within our Constitutional form of
republican government, yet masquerading itself with
the unmistakable brand of betrayal marked by
this generation of boomers whom have allowed bad
things to happen to this great nation. It can only
be explained as a *Moral Crisis!* Generations past did
not give themselves the liberty to do to others that
which is unlawful and evil to their neighbors since the
American Civil War and the Bankers of the Great
Depression. Individual private property was sacred.

In future titles, *I* will discuss the consequences
of social neglect upon the children who are given the
task and responsibility to be the Vanguards and
Trustees of this great nation! Do *we* dare do any less

for *them* than was done for *us?* The sacrifices made for the Boomer Generation Children? Can *we do* any less for the children and grandchildren of both the current and future generations! If not our duty to them, then who?

It is a fact that since the end of World War II, the traditional American heterosexual nuclear family has been ignored by the institutions of power within the United States of America.

This is affirmed by statistics that show since the generations since the second world war and specifically since the death of President Kennedy, the social norms have changed within the United States that has contributed greatly to the assault of the traditional nuclear family that the Republic was founded upon!

THE BALL DOCTRINE

It is unacceptable for this nation or *any* nation that believes that *family values* should be trashed by those in authority and power to affirm and protect them!

America's *moral compass* has been severely compromised by a generation of selfish, greedy and amoral people that the founder's of the nation would be *very angry* and shame! *We The People* have a moral duty to protect this nation given us by those who sacrificed and died to bring it to the world! Can *We The People* do any less for our children and grand children?

Those who are *tainted* by lust, greed, money, power and recognition and who will do anything to obtain them *are all damned* to death! God is *not* mocked for that which is *sown* shall also be *reaped!*[3]
[3]*Galatians 6:7 New Testament Bible*

THE BALL DOCTRINE

Since World War II, the boomer population has indulged in excesses that have hurt the traditional family structure within the United States and the World's populations. Western culture has mirrored indulgences that impersonate *those* of privilege and standing and create within the populations a *sense* of *ENTITLEMENT* that can only be satisfied by others.

As a consequence, the nation is in decline and with it, the World. *Human rights violations* are rampant along with prison populations filled with sociopaths and narcissists with many of those within the ranks of the *Judiciary and Law Enforcement* The abrogation of power for oneself, or one group brings with it the unmistakable betrayal of those who fought and died for them! Power, like a drug makes *us* its slave unless we make it our Accountable Servant!

THE BALL DOCTRINE

THE MORAL QUESTION?

The *moral* question for our time has always

been "H*ow sacred is life and property to any*

Generation?" During the Nazi occupation of Europe,

the confiscation of one's property, assets and human

rights were plundered, pilfered and pillaged by a

social elite of narcissists who valued nothing but their

own *desires* contrary to those of God and man. How

long did that go on? How long did the Communists

hold the Soviet Republic? How long will America

keep the ravages of *immorality and idolatry* of one's

personal property and human rights from becoming

thrown in the ash can of human history? God forbid

it not! To live under the grip of the State that would

destroy the individual rights and liberties of private

property owned by *its citizenry* is paramount to *death*

of this nation's foundations and sacrifice! God forbid it not! To have the moral equivalent of war waging class warfare within our own nation upon one's *life, liberty and personal property is absolutely contrary to the Rule Of Law, The Constitution and the intent of the Founders at the time of the Birth of this Nation!*

Tyranny, to hold the State and Federal Judiciary accountable for the evil they have both allowed and perpetuate within the Courts of this nation! I hold those who use, abuse and misuse *their* position and authority to hurt innocent parties from theft of their property and assets upon *those* that are *vulnerable adults and children* How in God's name can you live with yourselves for God is not mocked!

How in the name of God, can those who come from families think that they will gain by destroying their families legacy at the hands of third parties or in the alternative destroy other family members in their pursuit for their own selfish aims? How long do those who commit criminal acts against the innocent think they can go until one day they are stopped by their mental illness?

A Constitutional Republic requires strong families to know their rights and exercise them on a daily basis. It requires a quality of life that was created for the traditional family structure and *supported* by the "means in order to satisfy the ends".

When abuse replaces justice and neglect replaces equity then impunity by individuals replaces quality of life for which there is no equal! God forbid it not! *"Fore I know not what course others may take, but as for me, Give Me Liberty Or Give Me Death!"*[4]
Patrick Henry, March 23, 1775 - St John's Church, Richmond, VA,

3. THE FAMILY CRISIS!

"The Moral Test Of A Nation Is How A Nation

Finds Courage To Purge Evil From Itself

For The Sake Of It's Children & Family Structure"

If the traditional family structure is to survive as we have known it for hundreds if not thousands of years, it is incumbent that Society in coming years and centuries do something about it *NOW*!

Much time has been lost in the past ignoring a crisis that continues to grow as it gets worse each day from *Issues* important for its very survival go ignored and unattended. *What Are They?*

The crisis that afflicts the American traditional heterosexual nuclear family now has a long history of abuse dating back after the end of World War II that never became important enough to address until now!

THE BALL DOCTRINE

Society has morphed into a me, my and mine culture apart from its traditional family values ever since the end of World War II. How did this happen and what must be done about it? The issues are one and the same. Greedy politicians looking after their best interests and of others rather than those who matter most, our children, parents & grandparents, in other words us! *The Me must become the WE!*

It is a sad commentary on American life that the American people have allowed this tragedy to befall them as the world continues to change around us. Certainly, it is time to pay attention and do what is absolutely necessary for the sake of our heritage & our freedoms if we expect our children to survive and the children of future generations. NOW is the time for us to 'ask not what our country can do for us but what we can do for our United States Of America to secure the rights & freedoms we have known since the founding of the nation at the beginning of the Republic in 1776 for the sake of our current generation of children and those to come in the future.

Why is this important?

The history of the family in America has always affirmed one thing common to all generations until this one - "The Natural Order ".

This can be seen in nature that the animal kingdom supports itself in a chain of order structured to protect and preserve the natural family of each creation from Lions & Tigers to Beavers & Bears. The Natural Order speaks volumes how human beings are to live within a society of homogenous beings. As a consequence, it is unnatural for Society to stray from the traditional model of heterosexual nuclear family of mother, father and children. Anything less than the natural family order produces contradictions and conflicts for children raised in an unnatural family. The nation was founded upon the natural family and for *it* to survive, *it* must be preserved, protected and maintained as natural between a man and a woman, a mother and a father; not same sex!

This is a global problem but more importantly made worse by *Western Culture* particularly in the United States and Europe in recent years due to that *society in* general has ignored the traditional family and caused *it* to decline resulting in a culture crisis threatening the nation! The Natural Order of the heterosexual nuclear family is the dominant model *in nature* and worthy of being preserved & protected by *Western Society* in general; particularly within the United States Of America!

4. THE WORLD LEADERSHIP CRISIS!

Defined by time and distance, the United States of America has endured the ravages of political and social upheaval and unrest within its middle class by class warfare upon its institutions by the very children who are the product of the World War II Generation that fought for the nation's freedom that their families could continue to live under the 'Rule Of Law' within a Constitutional Republic. This *IS their legacy to preserve, protect and defend as the strength of the United States of America!*

However, it is now apparent that the World as we have known it has both shrunk and changed to the detriment of not only the traditional family in America, but the family structure around the World!

Nations are people and people are controlled by their *Society* either to their benefit or their detriment. In the case of the traditional family structure within the United States, the global reach of Asian nations led by China since the visit of Richard Nixon in 1972[5] has continued to show the world the power that economic change can have on nations both good and bad. Ultimately, economic and social change has a disproportionate affect on traditional families which has the potential to support or cause its demise.

It can be seen that within the last 40 years, the steady progression away from both individual liberty and family cohesiveness has exacted its toll on the children of the nation. Beginning with the repeal of the Glass Steagall Act by Bill Clinton, ratifying Free Trade Agreements and the assault on Marriage by the Gay Radical Left, American families have been left to confront assaults both personally and economically not since the American Civil War which divided the

(5) *Kissenger: 1973, The Crucial Year*

nation and families along party lines of economic slavery by an indentured class of *Black African Slaves* That crisis spilled over into civil violence on our own shores resulting in the deaths of over *750,000 soldiers* at the hands of their own brothers including the death of Abraham Lincoln.

The world as was known at the end of World War II has changed and with it has caused the nuclear family great stress in its quest to survive and thrive in a global economy. With a world in economic decline by some nations, <u>why</u> *and <u>what</u> must be done about it must be addressed, confronted and solved!*

Those in government leadership both inside and outside the United States are accountable to our children and future generations. As the world shrinks, more is expected of leaders to preserve, protect and defend our children from the assaults and threats in their best interests and those of our grandchildren!

World leaders have an *unprecedented opportunity* to cause their nations to respond to the global economic crisis by putting their children and families first by creating the "means of production to satisfy the ends" within their own country.

International economist, Hermando DeSoto[6] has traveled and studied the World Economies and has shown what can happen to make nations both *vital and independent* in their quest for *them* economically sound and socially cohesive. He traces beginnings, challenges and struggles for an emerging middle class societies and what and how they must do to make themselves prosperous and structurally sound. When economic principles are violated, disaster is often the product with greed, indifference and harm to the

[6] Hernando Desoto, Peruvian International Economist.

family structure. How this can be averted is the subject of a changing leadership within our World!

Why did this happen? *What* must be done about it? The economic decline of America is directly tied to the Corruption within Business, Labor and Government within the United States of America!

The *Social Contract* within American society is broken by *its leaders* placing undue stress upon its middle class families. The Social Contract extended after World War II allowing traditional American families not only to survive but to thrive within the United States. This Contract was defined by behavior that supported the *working middle class*, children and future generations. This lasted until the Corporate profits of big business overwhelmed ordinary citizens and their families to the extent that working families have had to scramble everyday in order to survive.

THE BALL DOCTRINE

Why did this happen and *What* must the nation do to recover from the paralyzing impact and toll it has on all of us? A bad economy creates economic and social problems for working class people for their families as unacceptable when Corporate profits rise at the expense of the working class.

How do we know this? The Bureau Of Labor Statistics tracked the history of Wages and Profits in America's economy since the end of World War II. Statistics show that American Gross National Product (GDP) rose at a steady rate while America's working class has only realized a 7% increase in wages and salaries. This is disproportionate and damaging to the traditional American family. *Who Is To Blame?*

Let us answer these important questions to better understand *what must be done about them!*

Like watching time, history shows us the truth.

THE BALL DOCTRINE

A case can be made that with economic gains, prosperity becomes a temptation to live extravagantly with an attitude of entitlement. This attitude can also be communicated to children and grandchildren and is very destructive to family unity and cooperation! An attitude of extravagance within a family unit has its roots in the leadership of the culture. *Who* is to blame? The Culture in the United States Of America!

This explains the *Why* for the economic decline within America and the *Who* that is responsible for it! While Americans have been working, the upper social classes have been *bullying and abusive   This must stop and this must change! Our children deserve better!*

To solve this crisis will require the finest minds that business, labor and government have to offer to assist the Social Contract for this culture to change.

THE BALL DOCTRINE

The cultural decline in America can be traced after the end of World War II. Though some historians place its beginning during the beginning period of the rise of the Nazi empire in Europe during the mid to late 1930's, it is generally agreed that the permissive and egocentric attitudes of the post World War II era contributed greatly to the economic, political and social upheaval with the United States and World politics; especially within the underdeveloped nations known as the Third World.

"I am going to make a statement you can take to the Bank and that is since the end of World War II, America and the World's problems have been created and were not necessary if the right attitude toward the traditional family had been adopted throughout the World and affirmed by the World's leaders "

Conflicts within the context of the Social Contract of Society has failed to move the nations to find ways to make their nations more productive, prosperous and peaceable within their own borders except for that of a few countries where families matter and the Social Contract within their community at large. These countries put their children first and make the family important within their own community. *Who Are They?*

Some are in Asia, others in Africa or Central and South America. Europe, America the Caribbean Island Nations who put a greater emphasis and their national heritage and history and desire that their children be fluent in knowing where they came from who they are and where they are going. In other words, a purpose driven life.

It is in this context that a World Leadership Crisis exists by which *an answer* is necessary to correct it. *What Is The Answer?*

5. <u>EVERY NATION AN ECONOMIC ENGINE!</u>

So far I have attempted to lay out my concerns that have impacted the nation and world. *Now,* the question must be answered how do we solve the global economic crisis with leaders who understand their role in the larger picture of global hegemony in a pluralistic society?

Like economists, I have studied the nations of the world to learn of their differences. There have always been differences amongst peoples of varying ethnic and social groupings throughout the history of our planet beginning with ancient civilizations.

All of them put an emphasis on their ability to keep their family structure in tact to provide for both themselves and their women and children. This is still the norm within society today. In that, nothing has changed except that *humanity* within society has not changed either. Not changed in terms of priorities that move *society* away from poverty into prosperity for all the nations of the earth; not just a few and the same ones who remain prosperous at the expense of others.

Economic stagflation is as cruel to a nation as hyper inflation. Each nation must become an economic engine in and of itself! This is the solution to the leadership problem. Make each nation take responsibility for itself to see that its children are secure by a solid work force of parents who benefit from the national emphasis to put them to work and make their family a productive part of the whole of society. This is known as "Adam Smith" Capitalism where the means satisfies the ends. This is the vision to move America away from being interdependent on the world to live and survive to being independent able to care for itself despite the products and services of others by producing the goods and services competitively priced within our own economy as the norm; not the exception!

THE BALL DOCTRINE

This should be our economic goal to preserve, protect and defend the nation from enemies both foreign and domestic including economic deprivation by stagflation draining our capital and making small business viable once again. *Jobs* are a product of economic policies that support family unity and not separate families by it.

To get America working may require a "Race To The Top"[7] where the nation competes with itself to create the means of production in order to satisfy the ends of "Adam Smith" Capitalism. A national jobs program would not hurt either including creating an Energy Security Trust[8] similar to the one the White House recently introduced at Argon, Illinois for the nation to finally get serious about producing energy that is environmentally friendly non polluting with technologies that build up society and make the

(7) MI Governor Jennifer Granholm, "A Governor's Journey."
(8) White House website WH.org "Energy Security Trust".

40

nuclear family economically stronger; not weaker!

If the Ball Doctrine means anything at all, it means that business, labor and government reset their priorities in the best interests of the traditional nuclear family structure and not their shareholders. Corporate capitalism devoid of making family issues a social priority is akin to cancer growing uncontrollably within the body politic. It doesn't work! Children require support and so do parents. For that to be tampered, altered and destroyed is akin to a disease that invades the body. It dies!

If the family dies in America, it will die all over the world because Corporate sponsorship of slave labor will have returned to the global economy including the United States which there is much evidence it is already here evident that some parents must work two or three different jobs in order to create enough money in order just to survive. This is a national tragedy created by society by

41

which there is no excuse!

As noted, I have attempted to explain that each nation must find within itself the economic relationships that they can build upon to benefit their own people, families and children.

The more diversified their economies the better moving forward on a number of issues and opportunities that may be afforded to them. From growing medicines, to growing wheat, grains & barley. Agriculture is a staple of the nations and provides much needed food nutrition by the development within their own national economies. The emphasis placed on the leadership of the nations. So goes the families of the nations so go the nations themselves.

Every nation an economic engine for its local trade, its local tourism, its local manufacturing, its local libraries, its local small business financing, farming, manufacturing from durable goods to pharmaceuticals, transportation and commodities. Every nation its own economic engine to root out poverty replaced by economic ingenuity that lifts their local economies and makes the traditional family unit not only survive but thrive within their own local economy

This is the magic of Capitalism that works in concert with the families within their own communities.

Investment from within and from without makes that possible. The International Monetary Fund has a major role to play in assisting and accomplishing this noble goal. Rooting out corruption at every level of local, state and national governments must be a goal of the people of the World!

Human beings were not made to live isolated lives but to live lives that are in harmony with their natural environment that was put here for them to use and not abuse. To do so, however, requires that those in power and authority understand abusive behavior by them, will not be tolerated by the laws of God and those laws given to man. Even now, in repressive times when nations act independently from the will of their own people, the laws of nature and of God are in motion to correct the immorality, brutality and tyranny that are created upon the innocent and vulnerable. For God is not mocked! For what a nation sows, it shall also reap!

Every nation an economic engine and in the next chapter I will discuss how to get there by creating the means in order to satisfy the ends!

6. <u>CREATING THE MEANS TO SATISFY THE ENDS!</u>

So far, I have discussed the economic and leadership crisis facing the Nation and World. As I see it, the current leadership is *inadequate* to cope with all the pressures created by nations who's leaders are devoid of moral courage to put the family first in their considerations and decisions that *will* change the course for the betterment of all mankind throughout the world. This then becomes the pressing issue of our time that to create stability in the Nation and World is to produce the "means to satisfy the ends" and not just for corporate stock holders but for individual families struggling to survive in a global economy both *near* and *far*

I compare this time to a period in American history during the American Civil War when writing to one of his colonels in the field, Abraham Lincoln wrote, "*I see in the near future a crisis approaching that unnerves me and causes me to tremble for the safety of my country corporations have been enthroned and an era of corruption in high places will follow, and the money power of the country will endeavor to prolong its reign by working upon the pre}udices of the people until all wealth is aggregated in a few hands and the republic is destroyed!*"[9]

What Lincoln saw *one hundred and fifty years* before the fact was the demise of the Republic because of greed from within and from without the United States. As a matter of fact, both the American Revolution of 1776 and the American Civil War of 1860 were created by the tension of economic interests detrimental to the American family structure. Lincoln saw this and wrote about it to his most trusted

(9) Abraham Lincoln, November 21, 1864 - In a letter to Colonel Wm. F. Elkins

commanders and leaders in the field.

America and its people can learn from history to not repeat the mistakes of the past but to move forward to the future by correcting the mistakes of past generations replacing them with time tested and proven policies, methods and procedures to insure future generations with the foundations for their success!

This is The Ball Doctrine to change the course of humanity and world history not only for the now generation but for those to come! To change it for the betterment of its children and those who's task it is to raise them, the parents and grandparents. Society has failed its children but society can change by deciding what is in the best interests of all its people and the traditional family structure. When that becomes the staple of social dialogue, then the "means to satisfy the ends" becomes much easier to find and do. Finding the means to satisfy the ends is an ongoing cyclical process to create and implement policies that benefit business, labor and government for them to do their job to support and build strong families for a strong democracy and constitutional republic. America is only as strong as its *moral* compass will allow it to lead the nation and the world.

It is easy to find *fault* amongst *her* people but also hope that change will come by people who know the difference and are willing to *motivate* themselves and others back into the culture to correct it by participating in the process of elections and good government on the local, state and federal level.

The culture must change for the benefit of its children for their future success and the success of their children. This is the story of our World!

THE BALL DOCTRINE

So goes the traditional heterosexual nuclear family so goes our World! As President Kennedy reminded us at his inaugural speech to ask "what we can do for our Country", let us also dedicate ourselves to stop a culture of corruption and abuse by holding those accountable who would use, abuse and misuse our rights to our own detriment and that of our children.

I cannot overemphasize the importance to all of the American people participating in the process of cultural change for the betterment of both individual liberty and family unity. Both fit like hand and glove.

Like Lincoln, my concerns are a World where the means must come to satisfy the ends for economic change. It is a fact that an inanimate object will not move until an external force is placed upon it. What is that force? The laws of *phy*sics are precise. The means must be created to satisfy the ends to support the nations of the world and its populations and children.   There are roughly *eight billion* people on planet earth. However, the United States only consists of less than *five percent* of it but consumes some *twenty percent* of its natural resources in consumer goods and energy. The cost to the nation is great and staggering and demands a review of its policies both monetary and fiscal to counter and correct the path it is on. This same review must be done by every industrial nation to save the planet from itself by *climate change* and to introduce products and services that will have a direct impact on that change.

Leadership is not cheap and neither is the history of the United States. I encourage everyone concerned with the current state of affairs in America to invest your time in learning our history & heritage so that it may be taught to our children and build in them an expectation of achievement and success in life that is rewarding and satisfying by business, labor and government working together to make that happen!

Every nation requires the support of business, labor and government within their own borders. This is the *challenge* to the nations in the 21st Century. To stem the tide of *violence* to make war by focusing the World's attention on the *productive* driven life of our nations doing the things that are productive, profitable and promising to enrich the lives of our children and their children for future generations.

The missing link in our dialogue and conversations as a Nation and World is the Best Interests of Children, Parents and Grand Parents. This is the traditional heterosexual nuclear family, the staple of society by which nations rise and fall on its vitality and support or lack thereof. The United States of America was founded on these principles & has served the Republic well for decades until others decided to change the dynamic of the family structure to suit their own agenda. This cannot be because *Society* is created in the image of God knowing good from evil making moral decisions knowing they are wrong but committing to them anyway.

The World is in a *cauldron* of conflicting ideas regarding the conduct and behavior that leads to the path of *Success!* Time tested foundations for generations that built America and created the means to satisfy and support the ends must return to the land of plenty once again! That will require all Americans to invest themselves in their family and see to it that they and their children are secure from business, labor and government of using, misusing and abusing them at the expense of our children and future generations!

My grandfather told my mother for him to raise his pigs he'd have to grow some corn on his farm. That always stuck with me as a child because it illustrates a principle that has been long tested and proven worthy that now *twenty three million American's who should be working contributing to the Social Security and Medicare funds can't because the "Means are not here to Satisfy the Ends!"*

Faith, Family & Future generations must hold fast to these truths that the Means must satisfy the ends; that without the "Means" to produce consumer goods and services, their can be no production to *satisfy* the ends. Without Vision and Initiative, there can be no solution to the complex problems that face the nation and the world. How does Society deal with such a Crisis?

As it always has been by evaluating its past to produce its future, Americans are some of the most productive people on the planet if not the most frugal of all the nations. Yet, Corporations have betrayed its people by allowing abuses that have negatively impacted traditional families setting them back and putting unnecessary burdens on us that should not be.

When I think of "good behavior" being punished for bad, I think how history repeats itself in the lives of our people. Immigrants who work hard but may not be rewarded for their efforts yet their bosses make big profits from their labor. I think of those in upper and lower management who have a duty to reward good behavior yet create obstacles for some of their most productive workers that works against them and ultimately the success of their family structure.

"Racing To The Top" by competing for new products and innovations within your own country, creating government partnerships by encouraging small business development and funding by local, state and federal government. Remember, no official ever spent one dime or penny that someone else did not earn. Therefore, wasteful government spending is unacceptable and there are a host of programs that need and should be cut. Those that hold promise and formidable for production of durable goods should be funded, but most if not all secondary projects should be cut and there budgets with them. Invest in durable goods that support the traditional family world wide and you master the art of supporting your children and their future! Their parents will thank you and so

THE BALL DOCTRINE

will *Society The means must satisfy the ends in order*

to make society sustainable and their economy viable

Without the means there can be no ends only poverty.

7. NO CHILD LEFT BEHIND!

Now, we have launched the sacred divide that nations seldom tread for out of fear that their rulers would not follow but rather abstain from acting in the best interests of their own people. This is the story of humanity from hence civilization as we have known came. The abuse wrought down on America and its people is both from within and without. The Founders were *wary* that indifference by the *electorate* toward public policy would be the undoing of a strong nation and democracy by which the young nation had many growing pains to breach and overcome.

This then is the issue that continues into the 21st Century America. It is Incredible to me that throughout the history of the World, philosophers, historians, policy makers, Kings, Queens, Priests, Popes, Ruling Elites, including religious figures except for one has failed to show the World by what and how they are to conduct human affairs amongst themselves, their children and families.

It is my fervent prayer I offer that human beings will decide to change their behavior for the best interests of their children and families. This is the Natural Order that says to all of us, "No Child Left Behind!

This also applies to *abortion* not as a means of contraception nor a means of taking and denying human life. All children are precious in the sight of God from which they come. There can be no doubt that the genetics created in human beings came from a higher power to sustain and maintain. Should we not respect and obey the Natural Order that life has seen fit to establish within the traditional heterosexual family unit? Do we know more than the Creator?

THE BALL DOCTRINE

What needs to happen is that the people of the World decide that families are important enough to invest their time and treasure to preserve, protect and defend! Each child born in this World deserves a chance at life!

And that life requires the support of those within and without their own community.

8. <u>EVERY AMERICAN ACCOUNTABLE!</u>

Now, the test of time continues to test America and its Will to preserve, protect and defend national institutions designed to support the traditional family structure to keep it strong and provide for the common defense of its Children, Parents, and Grand Parents. Is that too hard to understand?

For hundreds of years, that has been the standard and for hundreds to come it will remain the standard and not the exception in spite of those who denigrate, demonstrate and defecate on the Constitution, Bill Of Rights and Rule Of Law. America is a Constitutional Republic governed by laws designed to support the traditional heterosexual nuclear family. That is what America was destined to become and lead the World!

Those who would conspire to defeat America are

enemies of the State and must be dealt with regardless of their position or power within American Society. The doctrine that enemies of the State both foreign & domestic within and without the United States have safe harbor is an anomaly and throw back to the American Revolution where by Patriots saw the problem of living in a Society of Unaccountable Citizens given to supporting a Government of Corruption paying their tax dollars to those given to using, abusing and misusing them for personal profit and privilege. In other words, "Taxation Without Representation" which is what America is today!

The Ball Doctrine, says "Enough!" of the abuse that plagues our Cities, towns and municipalities! Yes, Private Citizens, not lawyers with an interest in Public Service with term limits who know and support their families, communities and government by the sweat of their brow and by the stress of their body and the anxiety created by *unnatural and overwhelming demands* placed upon them to produce for themselves and those they love.

These are the leaders missing in Local, State & Federal Government! These are the Patriots that must show up *NOW*! To lead the nation and the World to a new policy that Business, Labor & Government act in the BEST INTERESTS of Children, Parents & Grand Parents consistent with the Rule Of Law and the best traditions of the Traditional Heterosexual Nuclear family creating the Means Of Production to Satisfy the ends! The Ball Doctrine applies to all nations for their families to show the World a better way to live and defeat the forces of EVIL that would destroy it!

9. AMERICA'S MANIFEST DESTINY, FOREIGN DEBT & THE COMMERCE CLAUSE!

"He That Is Good At Making Excuses Is Seldom

Good For Anything Else" - Ben}amin Franklin

"If Men Were Angels, No Government Would Be

Necessary If Angels Were To Govern Men, Neither

External Nor Internal Controls On Government

Would Be Necessary In Framing A Government

Which Is To Be Administered By Men Over Men,

The Great Difficulty Lies In This: You Must First

Enable The Government To Control The Governed;

In The Next Place Oblige It To Control Itself "

President James Madison: The Federalist Papers No 51

THE BALL DOCTRINE

"IF AN ARAB NATION IMPOSES SHARIA LAW ON ITS OWN PEOPLE, THE GOVERNMENT OF THAT NATION BECOMES A DICTATOR OF THE PEOPLE! THE UNITED STATES CANNOT FUND THAT NATION WHILE THE PEOPLE LIVE UNDER THE RULES THEY DID NOT WANT OR APPROVE DEMOCRACY IN THE MIDDLE EAST REQUIRES THE PEOPLE TO CHOOSE THEIR CONSTITUTION & RULE OF LAW"

-DENNIS ANDREW BALL-
AMERICAN FOREIGN POLICY

"IT WILL BE OF LITTLE AVAIL TO THE PEOPLE,

THAT THE LAWS ARE MADE BY MEN OF THEIR

OWN CHOICE, IF THE LAWS BE SO

VOLUMINOUS

THAT THEY CANNOT BE READ, OR

INCOHERENT THAT THEY CANNOT BE

UNDERSTOOD "- PRESIDENT JAMES MADISON, THE FEDERALIST PAPERS NO 62

THE BALL DOCTRINE

Now, the expressions made by those who made the policies that made and sustained the nation must be revisited and made to work once again!

The Ball Doctrine affirms America's Manifest Destiny that propelled the nation to be the leader in the World to assist its families and provide for the common defense. American foreign policy must lead the world to an awareness that family life and democratic principles of life, liberty and the pursuit of happiness are universal principles of civil society; something the founders understood and wrestled with just as all nations wrestle with their reality at home and abroad.

Foreign Debt is a product of nations who cause the American people to pay for security from enemies of the State who abuse, misuse and use our tax dollars and burn our flag! Why? Because since the end of World War II, President Dwight Eisenhower warned America of the Industrial Military Complex with their compulsion to spend, spend, spend for projects that may or may not be necessary including the funding of wars since that time.

America's manifest destiny was a doctrine used at a time in the nation's history to assist and expand the nation through Indian territory while the federal government and those in Congress charted a path to bring the nation together and strengthen the families that it served. The issues all of us struggle have their roots in the behavior fought and died to make America a nation where one's private property and liquidity was considered sacred to the individual and their family by which it was created and sustained. That no longer exists in the United States Of America and is a tragedy that must be reversed!

America was founded upon the notion that one's

private property was no one's property but that of the owner and that the State could not unilaterally dispense or have claim to it without the consent of the owner for it.

It should be known that this reality applies to foreign country's that wish to exploit and use America's weakness to spend it's economy to the detriment of its governed tax payers to their advantage by creating scenario's that places foreign debt in opposition to American Sovereignty.

Throughout our history, it is a fact that America's interests where always the Public Interest. That in spite of greedy robber barons, family hegemony and personal accountability with integrity was the character of American Society. We were once a nation of heroes. We still can be heroes to our families and provide the common defense. But we must be smart and act in the best interests of those who value our way of life and desire to preserve and protect it. That is being a Trustee of the nation which

THE BALL DOCTRINE

as citizens, we are all called to be. Let us not forget that the reason's for America's decline is a product of neglect and greed by those who control Business, Labor and Government to the detriment of the sustainability of the traditional working family.

Let us also not forget that America's manifest destiny to prosper and grow was a work in progress. It still is. But the difference now is that we live in a 21st Century Society of Global Proportions where by nations compete to sustain their economies and in many cases abuse the other to gain an unfair advantage to prosper at their trading partners and that nation's expense. This is a violation by our leaders to compromise and deal at the people's expense when in the Public Interest it is our leaders' duty to protect American property and Sovereignty that cannot be taken by foreign debt, especially from China. The founder's warned not to become entangled by controls of currency by loans. This was most evident early in the nation's history when in 1829-37, President Andrew Jackson fought the Bank of the United States controlled by European Banking interests; shut it down! He fought the bank and became a target by powerful financial interests to end his presidency.

However, he did prevail and paid off the bank debt of seven million dollars. The only President that ever paid off the national debt with the Federal Treasury because it was important that America's Sovereignty be protected from enemies both foreign and domestic. Remember that!

The United States Of America is not a Bank! We are a Constitutional Republic! With laws applicable to all! Every nation should be modeled to serve its people and the people to create the means to satisfy the ends! That's whats missing in our World and has for generations! That's real change; something that must come of age!

THE BALL DOCTRINE

It's time the nation lead the World back to our roots and foundations for generations! The Children of the World deserve to live with parents who love them and a society that cares for them. The economics must work for them in order for them to not only survive but thrive! That's America's Manifest Destiny keeping our nation sovereign and providing for the common defense!

THE COMMERCE CLAUSE:

Article 1, Section 8, Clause 3 of the Constitution Of The United States has allowed the Congress of the United States to compromise American interests both domestic & abroad by a very liberal interpretation of the act including the formation of the Interstate Commerce Act and the Sherman Anti-Trust Act.

Because domestic and foreign debt is now a national problem, the Commerce Clause **must** be defined to limit the power of the State to destroy American Sovereignty by foreign debt. Do you think nations America has borrowed do not want to own our Country? How easy to gain the very property they would go to war to obtain! Is that what you want America? To be owned by foreigners?

GET BUSY PEOPLE!

I ask you who's responsibility is it to secure the common defense for the United States? It is us! Why? Because We control the electoral process and our elected representatives regardless of party!

Legally, it is the Commerce Department and the President who make decisions by the Commerce Clause that impact our lives either good or bad. We have skin in this game! Because the quality of our lives in directly affected! And the Congress has the responsibility to see that the interests of the people are protected by them. However, if we the People fail to do our job in communicating what is unacceptable,

71

then we have failed our job to keep them honest and to protect our nation from threats of domination by foreign nations because of the debt we owe them. The founders where very concerned that a foreign nation would not have to fire a shot to own the United States! Is that what you want?

Get busy people! We must create the means of production to satisfy the ends. We must shrink our government's debt by shrinking the size of government. Ronald Reagan said it well "The problem we face is that government is not a solution to our problem but that government IS the problem!"[10] The problems they created for the American People are a direct result of what President James Garfield spoke at a time when America was at its infancy and needed a parent!

[10]"Now more than ever before, the people are responsible for the character of their Congress. If that body be ignorant, reckless and corrupt, it is because the people tolerate ignorance, recklessness and corruption." *President James Garfield(1881)*

THE BALL DOCTRINE

Our nation continues to suffer by a culture that has fallen down and allowed themselves to be corrupted at the hands of selfish, greedy and corrupt people! This is the State of our World. What are We going to do about it? Let's all get to work for the sake of our children, our families and our World! You know it and I know it and so do the people of the World!

Bill Clinton repealed the Glass-Steagall Act that protected America from unscrupulous bankers for 70 years. George W. Bush did nothing to restore it! Neither has Barack Obama! Why not?

Bill Clinton introduced the North American Free Trade Agreement (NAFTA). George W. Bush did nothing to repeal it. Barack Obama either. Why?

Bill Clinton allowed after Ronald Reagan illegal immigration to run wild! So did George W. Bush and Barack Obama! The Border States have responded because the federal government acted

impotent to the growing domestic crisis created by

the federal government to control it. As a result, the

nation has economically and domestically suffered by

by what Ronald Reagan said that government IS the

problem! As a consequence, the nation is in Crisis!

Illegals need not stay in the United States

unless they have a green card, become resident aliens,

return to Mexico or Country of Origin. The United

States is NOT a Bank! This was the intent of the

founders that immigrants come to the United States

legally through the immigration process established

by law. Every country including Mexico has their

own laws to be complied and so does the United

States!

It is estimated that over 11,000,000 illegal aliens

have been unlawfully allowed to occupy the United States with the American tax payer footing the bill for their support. Is that right for the working families of America? Do illegals contribute to the support of America's families? Important questions that have been largely ignored by Congress since amnesty was given to three million illegal aliens by President Reagan in 1986. This led to the election of Barak Obama because for every illegal alien given amnesty, five people under the family unification act allowed some 13,000,000 additional voters to elect Obama.

This is how America is being corrupted by an inept Congress and leadership from the Baby Boomer and subsequent generations! This cannot be sustained without a major correction within society! The founders provided that correction by action from

THE BALL DOCTRINE

WE THE PEOPLE! The Children and families of America deserve better from the sacrifices born by previous generations to insure domestic tranquility and the common defense. Any governmental agency that opposes the Constitutional guarantees afforded the legal citizens of the United States runs afoul of the Constitution and are considered *Rogue* officials subject to treason and imprisonment under the laws of the United States Of America and the Constitution by which an Oath they took to uphold!

10. <u>THE DESTINY OF A WORLD GONE GLOBAL!</u>

So far our attention has been on the family model we've known for hundreds if not thousands of years. All were affirmed in the belief that it was God who blesses America and who we acknowledge as our creator and giver of life, liberty and pursuit of happiness.

We also have spoken about the importance of preserving and protecting the BEST INTERESTS of the traditional heterosexual nuclear family, mothers, fathers and grandparents.

It is also true for all nations to consider the importance of these issues for their people and the matter of sustainability for their children and family structure.

We have discussed the means in order to satisfy

the ends for all nations for their welfare and future generations. Obviously, wars are created by nations and individuals who use, abuse and misuse their position and power for themselves rather than for their children. However, a strong defense is an effective deterrent to aggression by rogue states.

Therefore, it is the position of this Author, that nations use technology for peaceful purposes and only employ lethal force when attacked or to prevent or defend their vital interests that impact the security of their children and nation.

The United States has a golden opportunity to lead a World gone Global by introducing and affirming policy that supports traditional family life and recognizes that all people throughout the world confront many of the same needs, wants and desires not only to survive but thrive within a Global economy.

Poverty, ignorance and control have always been the enemies for positive social change within the nations of the world. That must change! Each nation must become sufficient to support itself with products, services or ideas that can be organized in a lawful and productive manner to support family life within their own economy and society without infringing upon the rights and needs of others.

The need for positive social change will become more evident as societies throughout the world demand that their rights be affirmed and that power be transferred to the needs of the people and family.

Let ALL of us embrace this and make it a reality for our children and future generations!

ABOUT THE AUTHOR

Dennis Andrew Ball is Chairman of the American

National Committee aka ANC since 1995 and continues to

usher Independent Leadership that reflects the conduct of

the Founding Fathers of the United States of America.

His leadership includes forming the American Party Of

America aka AOA at a time the nation was changing

economically and its negative impact on the traditional

heterosexual nuclear family. An American Patriot,

Dennis Andrew Ball is a

2016 Candidate for President Of The United States!

AMERICA 2000: Foundations For Generations!

was released in early 2012 and is the flagship book which

continues to be ordered both domestic and internationally.

Born August 27, 1951 in Los Angeles, California, Mr. Ball

is a "Natural Born Citizen" eligible to run for President

of the United States by Section 2 Article 1 of The

THE BALL DOCTRINE

Constitution Of The United States. He also holds a degree
from the University of California San Diego with
emphasis on Chinese History, Science & Technology.

Mr. Ball believes that World History will record that a
Third Party rose to meet the demands of today's Society to
interrupt the negative flow of energy to make it positive
once again for both the children of the current generations
and those future generations still waiting to impact the
traditional heterosexual nuclear family.

Your continued financial and moral support are necessary

for our time and our children!

Thank you!

www.ingramcontent.com/pod-product-compliance
Lightning Source LLC
Chambersburg PA
CBHW050559280326
41933CB00011B/1910